BOOKS BOOKS BOOKS

Celebrating 24 years of
Mick & Brita

The publishers and authors would like to thank Robert Davies
of the British Library for his invaluable assistance.

First published in Great Britain in 2017 by
Otter-Barry Books, Little Orchard, Burley Gate, Hereford, HR1 3QS

www.otterbarrybooks.com

A catalogue record for this book is available from the British Library.

ISBN 978-1-91095-998-5

Illustrated with collage, watercolour and digital art
www.mickandbrita.com

Printed in China

1 3 5 7 9 8 6 4 2

BOOKS
BOOKS
BOOKS

MICK MANNING & BRITA GRANSTRÖM

Explore Inside the
GREATEST
Library on Earth

Otter-Barry BOOKS
www.otterbarrybooks.com

CONTENTS

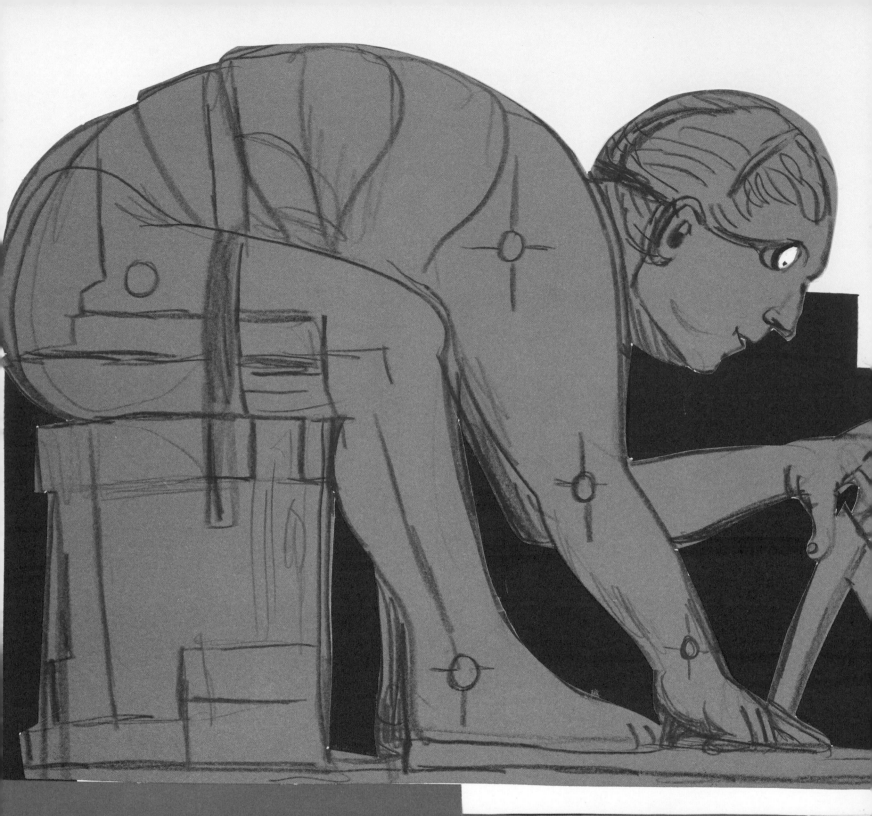

WELCOME to the greatest library in the world! We're going to take you on an amazing tour of its treasures – including some that are so rare they are kept under lock and key!

Welcome

The British Library, in London, is the national library of the United Kingdom and the largest public building to be constructed in the UK in the 20th century. It was built between 1988 and 1998, using 10 million bricks and 180,000 tonnes of concrete. Inside it has 625km (400 miles) of shelves, which would stretch almost from London to Edinburgh! And when you stand on the ground floor, there are nine floors above your head and five floors beneath your feet. **It's a giant** – just like Eduardo Paolozzi's sculpture of the famous scientist, Isaac Newton, in the courtyard.

The British Library holds one of the largest collections of books, prints, letters, drawings, maps, stamps, newspapers, plays and music in the world... over 150 million items, from the earliest printed books to books printed this year. So the British Library collection is a unique history of the book.

Are you ready to go inside?

Let's begin at the beginning, with
ancient, hand-made books like
THE ST CUTHBERT GOSPEL,
found in a coffin!

INMUNDU
INMUND
pep
et
l

Neq
sed ex
t uerbum
let babitauit inn

os omnes
gratiam pro g

The Gospel was originally placed in St Cuthbert's coffin at Lindisfarne Priory in Northumberland some time after his death in 687AD.

Later, it travelled with the saint's body as it was moved around the north of England to avoid the invading Vikings. The coffin was finally buried in Durham Cathedral.

The saint's Gospel was taken out of the coffin in the 1100s and later fell into private hands, until in 2011 the British Library bought it for nine million pounds!

The St Cuthbert Gospel, which contains the Gospel of St John, is the oldest surviving book in Europe to have its original covers and binding.

cepi 'uri nodio dissus ado
xtia cui nomen erat iohannes
bic uenit intestimo

And look at this – the magnificent
LINDISFARNE GOSPELS,
hand-lettered and painted by a monk
named Eadfrith over one thousand
three hundred years ago.

This beautiful book, containing all four
Gospels, is presumed to be the work of
Eadfrith, a Bishop of Lindisfarne and a
gifted artist and scribe. It was made
around 700AD in honour of St Cuthbert.
The original cover, decorated with jewels,
was stolen by Viking raiders.

imago leonis

ÓAGI
HA
R

US
CUS

Then there are stories about some of the
earliest super-heroes, like the Swedish warrior,
BEOWULF – a hero so strong he tore off a
man-eating monster's arm in single combat!

Beowulf comes to help a
Danish king, whose men are
being attacked by a man-eating
monster known as Grendel.

Beowulf lies in wait for Grendel
and, in a brutal wrestling match,
he tears off the monster's arm.
Grendel flees, bleeding to death.

Grendel's mother is even
fiercer! But Beowulf tracks her
to the bottom of a lake and
kills her with a sword.

Beowulf is the oldest surviving long poem in Old English. The British Library's copy, 3,000 lines long, was handwritten in the 11th century. Set in Scandinavia, and brought over to Britain by Anglo-Saxon settlers, the poem is a thrilling adventure story which would originally have been told out loud at feasts and gatherings.

Here is the famous Magna Carta, a historic promise to be just and fair – sealed by King John of England.

Magna Carta became an important part of English law and our laws today are still based on it. When the United States won independence from Britain, *Magna Carta* even influenced the US Constitution and Bill of Rights.

English nobles became fed up with King John's unfair punishments, heavy taxes and land-grabbing, to raise money for a war he was losing in France. So they decided to rebel.

To avoid a rebellion, a legal document was drawn up to say what the king could and could not do. *Magna Carta* means 'the Great Charter' and it was sealed, unwillingly, by King John in 1215 at Runnymede, beside the river Thames.

And here is **The Canterbury Tales,** by Geoffrey Chaucer, the very first book ever printed in English, using an amazing invention: movable type and a printing press!

Until the 15th century all books in Europe were handwritten, usually in Latin, but in 1436 the printing press was invented in Germany. William Caxton brought one to Britain in 1476 and with it he printed, in English, *The Canterbury Tales*, a brilliantly written collection of entertaining stories about a group of pilgrims travelling to Canterbury Cathedral. Shown here is a picture from *The Knight's Tale*, the story of two brave and honourable knights, who both fall in love with the same lady and fight a courtly duel to decide who will marry her.

There are **BIG** books, like this ginormous atlas made for King Charles the Second, THE KLENCKE ATLAS. It's so heavy it takes six people to lift it!

This book of maps was printed in Holland and presented to Charles II in 1660. It has 37 maps showing all parts of the world known to Europeans at that time, and when opened out it measures 1.78 x 2.1 metres!

And there are tiny books such as *Lady Jane Grey's Prayer Book.*
It might make you feel sad.

Lady Jane Grey was a great-niece of Henry VIII and she ruled as Queen of England for only nine days before Henry's daughter, Mary, took power. Jane was imprisoned and sentenced to death, aged only 17. She carried this little handwritten book to her execution, and it even has some of her own scribbled messages in the margins. The book measures just 85 x 70 millimetres.

Some books in the British Library, such as the First Folios of **William Shakespeare**, are so valuable they are kept in bomb-proof strong-rooms, deep underground.

William Shakespeare grew up in the age of Queen Elizabeth I. As a young man, he left his home town of Stratford-upon-Avon to work in the new theatres that were springing up in London. Shakespeare went on to become the world's greatest dramatist, writing many unforgettable plays, including *Romeo and Juliet*, *A Midsummer Night's Dream*, *Hamlet* and *Macbeth*.

Alas, poor Yorick!

The graveyard scene from *Hamlet*

The First Folio was the first full collection of Shakespeare's plays to be printed in 1623. Eighteen of the 36 plays had never been printed before, so without the First Folio some of the finest plays in the world might have been lost forever.

O speak again, bright angel!

The balcony scene from *Romeo and Juliet*

TOFFEE, RUSSIAN.

INGRÉDIENTS.—¼ of a lb. of loaf sugar, ¾ of a pint of cream, flavouring.

METHOD.—Dissolve the sugar in the cream, stand the stewpan in a bain-marie or tin of boiling water, and stir and cook until the mixture thickens and leaves the sides of the pan. Remove from the fire, stir in the flavouring essence, pour on to oiled or greased tins, and when cold cut into squares.

Are you hungry after all that drama? Do you fancy a cod shoulder or a sheep's head? There are enough COOKERY BOOKS in the British Library to give you serious tummy-ache!

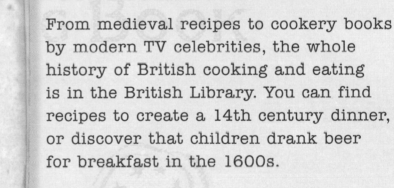

From medieval recipes to cookery books by modern TV celebrities, the whole history of British cooking and eating is in the British Library. You can find recipes to create a 14th century dinner, or discover that children drank beer for breakfast in the 1600s.

Mrs Isabella Beeton was the superstar cookbook writer of Victorian times. Her *Book of Household Management*, published in 1861, was a huge bestseller. More than a cookbook, it gives advice on everything from cleaning the silver to getting rid of rats!

Still got tummy-ache? Well, there are **MEDICAL BOOKS** too – but some of the older books in the British Library's collection might make you feel even worse!

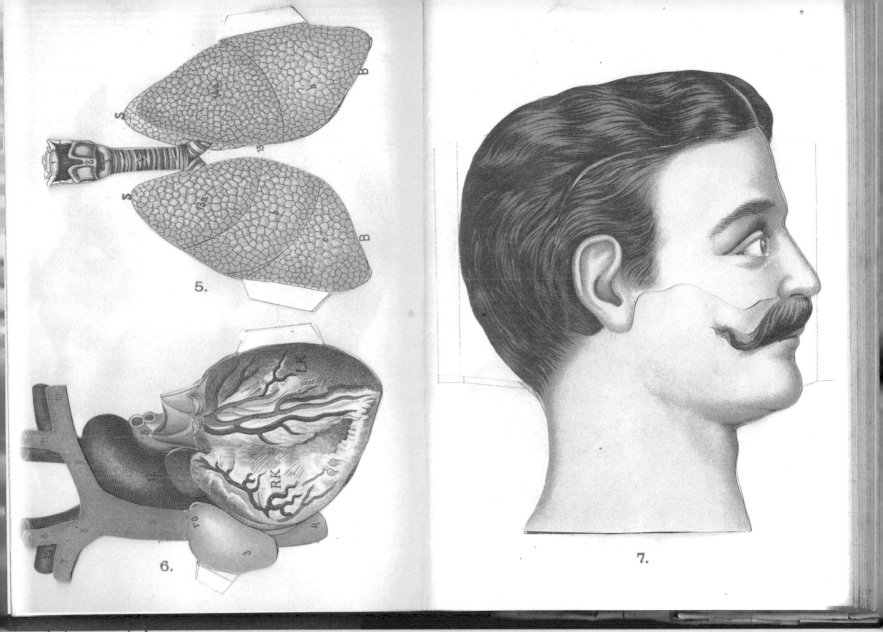

5.

6.

7.

People come from all over the world to the British Library to find some of the best – as well as the strangest – books on medicine. A Scottish doctor in the 18th century, Charles Alston, described how the juice of squashed woodlice could be taken to cure children's colic, in his book *Lectures on the Materia Medica* (1770).

Amazing fold-outs and paper engineering appear when you open *The New Natural Healing Method*, by the pioneering nineteenth-century doctor Friedrich Bilz.

Look out for the works of great women writers such as *Jane Austen*, and her witty, clever books about love, pride and jealousy among the English gentry.

Jane Austen wrote her stories in the early 1800s. Her six wonderful novels are full of lively characters, intrigues and romances, from *Sense and Sensibility*, about two sisters seeking love in very different ways, to *Emma*, a funny but touching story about a headstrong girl who tries unsuccessfully to do some match-making for her friend!

Here is the 15-year-old Jane Austen writing her *History of England*, which makes fun of the usual kind of boring history book which children had to read in those days. Jane's sister, Cassandra, drew the pictures.

PRIDE & PREJUDICE
by JANE AUSTEN

With twenty-four coloured illustrations
by C.E.BROCK

In Jane Austen's most famous story, *Pride and Prejudice*, we meet Mr Darcy, the arrogant upper-class gentleman who learns he has been too proud, and Elizabeth Bennet, the clever girl with whom he falls in love, along with the rest of the Bennet sisters and their comic, foolish mother – plus a villainous soldier!

Elizabeth Bennet first meets rich Mr Darcy at a ball but is offended by his proud, unfriendly manner.

Mr Darcy finally reveals a secret to Elizabeth, which shows his true character.

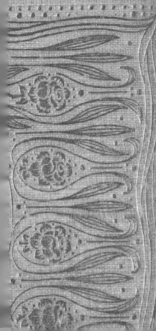

And let's look at the handwritten stories, letters and novels of the three extraordinary **Brontë sisters**, living and writing in a parsonage on the wild Yorkshire moors almost 200 years ago.

Emily Brontë's *Wuthering Heights*, set on the moors, tells a dramatic story of the violence and passion between Cathy and Heathcliff.

Charlotte Brontë's *Jane Eyre* shows how Jane survives harsh schooldays to become an independent young woman who, as a governess, falls in love with her boss, Mr Rochester.

Anne Brontë's *The Tenant of Wildfell Hall* is about a married woman brave enough to leave her abusive husband and take her child with her.

Victorian readers were both shocked and thrilled by the Brontë sisters' revolutionary stories about strong female characters.

ERING HEIGHTS

A NOVEL.

JANE EYRE

BY CHARLOTTE BRONTË

THOMAS CAUTLEY NE
72, MORTIMER ST.,

GEORGE ROUTLEDG

And there are books by brothers, too.
THE BROTHERS GRIMM roamed the
Black Forest in Germany 200 years ago, looking
for tales of wicked witches and cruel queens.

Brothers Wilhelm and Jakob Grimm collected word-of-mouth fairy
stories such as Hansel and Gretel, Snow White and Rapunzel from
country folk and wrote them down. Without the books of the Brothers
Grimm, these magical stories could have been forgotten and lost forever.

What about the wonderful stories of **Charles Dickens**?
Charles began work at the age of 12 in a boot-polish factory but later became one of the greatest storytellers of all time.

A CHRISTMAS CAR

BY
S DICKENS

ILLUSTRATED BY
ARTHUR RACKHAM

LONDON
PHILADELPHIA

WILLIAM HEINEMANN
J.B. LIPPINCOTT Cº

Price 1s.

MARCH.

BLEAK HOUSE

LIFE AND ADVENTURES
OF
NICHOLAS NICKLEBY

CONTAINING
A FAITHFUL ACCOUNT OF THE
Misfortunes, Uprisings, Downfallings,
AND
CAREER OF THE NICKLEBY FAMILY

Charles Dickens' many novels, all
written in the 19th century, championed
the poor and homeless, and exposed the
evils of child labour. In *Oliver Twist*,
a poor orphan gets caught up in a
criminal gang and in *The Old Curiosity
Shop*, Little Nell and her grandpa have
to leave their beloved shop and become
homeless beggars.

When poor Oliver Twist
asks for more gruel in the
workhouse, he is cruelly
punished.

Little Nell and her grandpa
have to say goodbye to their
home, the Old Curiosity Shop,
for ever.

But the
British Library
doesn't just boast great
storytellers. It proudly
celebrates the greatest scientific
minds of all time, with
treasures like the notebooks
of the artist and inventor,
*Leonardo
da Vinci.*

This collection of drawings and notes shows us the workings of Leonardo's amazing and ambitious mind. He lived in the 15th century, but even now his designs are helping scientists develop machines to be used in possible future landings on the planet Mars!

Leonardo wrote backwards in his notebooks, maybe to keep them secret but more likely because he could, and found it funny!

And there are nature books, like this one by the 18th century writer Oliver Goldsmith.

Of course the genius **Charles Darwin** is here, too. His five-year voyage round the world 200 years ago led him to make tremendous discoveries about evolution in his 1859 masterwork, *On the Origin of Species*.

Oliver Goldsmith's hugely popular *A History of the Earth, and Animated Nature*, first published in 1774, was republished in 1824, illustrated with many beautiful engravings.

Darwin was inspired to write *On the Origin of Species* after his five-year world voyage as a young scientist aboard HMS Beagle. The book challenged the traditional view of how the world was created, with discoveries about how animal species had evolved over time, including the revolutionary idea that humans were descended from apes.

After all that science, what about something very unscientific – Lewis Carroll's unforgettable story of a little girl called Alice, who falls down a rabbit hole and discovers a magical world...

Alice's Adventures in Wonderland.

ALICE'S
ADVENTURES IN
WONDERLAND

she found

The Queen of Hearts

All on a summ

ve of Hearts
took them

the eviden
ence.»
fl

Alice's Adventures in Wonderland is about a little girl who shrinks and travels to the weird and fantastic world of Wonderland to meet a White Rabbit, a sleepy Dormouse, a Mad Hatter, a crazy Queen of Hearts and lots of other amazing characters. It was written in 1865 and not only changed the way many people thought about children's books but was read by many adults too.

If you prefer facts to fantasy, catch up on the news with over 60 million **NEWSPAPERS** – including the first ever copy of *The Times*.

The Times was first printed in 1788. Alongside politics and news about the trials of highwaymen, there were theatre and opera announcements and lots of advertisements. Can you spot the 'ad' for a book about horse-riding skills? In the eighteenth century it was the equivalent of learning to drive a car!

Or how about a concert with handwritten sheet music to make you sing and dance? This is the explosive *Music for the Royal Fireworks* by Handel.

Handel could erupt like a firework himself. His rages were famous. Once he threw a kettledrum at the leader of an orchestra so hard that his wig fell off.

George Frideric Handel's *Music for the Royal Fireworks* was first performed in the open air, in London, in 1749. Handel's handwritten score is part of the British Library's vast music collection, which includes work by thousands of world-famous composers.

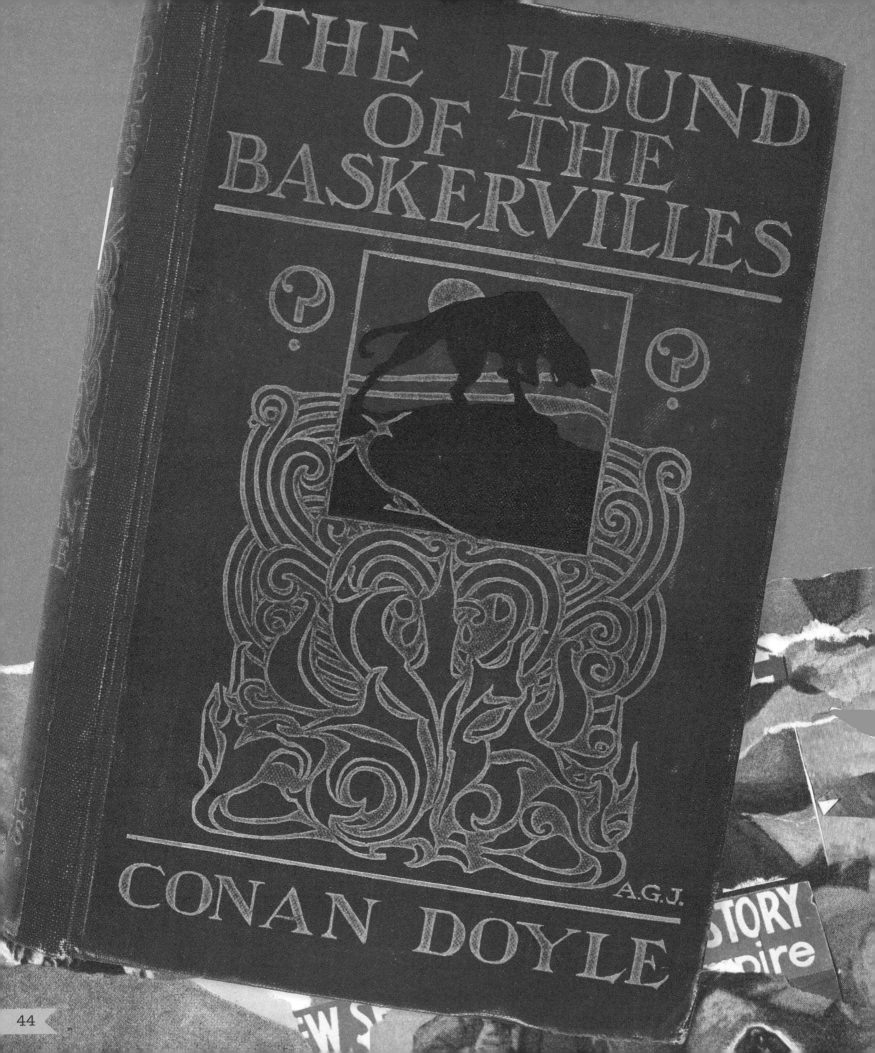

Feeling tired after all that? How about an adventure story before bedtime? Join the super-sleuth SHERLOCK HOLMES and his faithful friend, Doctor Watson, as they track down the Hound of the Baskervilles.

Sir Arthur Conan Doyle is most famous for his renowned series of detective adventures featuring the eccentric genius, Sherlock Holmes, and his loyal side-kick, Doctor Watson.

In *The Hound of the Baskervilles*, published in 1902, Holmes and Watson try to solve a terrifying mystery on lonely Dartmoor. Not only is an escaped prisoner on the loose but a giant, savage dog is terrorising the moor!

We hope you enjoyed your tour of the BRITISH LIBRARY and some of its treasures. The Library receives a copy of every single book published in the United Kingdom and Ireland – including this one! When you order a book to look at, it travels to you from the vaults on an automatic conveyor system, like a little railway. Find out about British Library events and exhibitions at www.bl.uk

Almost every country in the world has a National Library. The Library of Congress in Washington, USA, claims to be the largest of all. Founded in 1800, it holds over 162 million items. Australia's National Library, in Canberra, is much younger, founded in 1960, but already has over ten million items. However, libraries don't have be huge to have great books. Perhaps there is a public lending library near you? Go and support your local libraries, and see for yourself what exciting places they are.

MORE ABOUT THE WORKS AND THEIR AUTHORS:

THE ST CUTHBERT GOSPEL – This book, which contains the Gospel of St John, is tiny, with a page size of only 138 x 92 millimetres. It is handwritten in Latin, in beautiful script.

THE LINDISFARNE GOSPELS – This book was hand-lettered and painted on vellum (calfskin), and contains the Gospels of St Matthew, St Mark, St Luke and St John. The picture shows a winged lion from the Gospel of St John.

BEOWULF – The copy in the British Library is unique and so extremely fragile that it has to be looked after very carefully in case it crumbles away.

MAGNA CARTA – The other earliest copies of this ancient legal agreement are kept at Salisbury and Lincoln Cathedrals.

GEOFFREY CHAUCER – Chaucer was a royal courtier and a diplomat. His groundbreaking books were so important that he became known as the 'father of English literature', influencing future writers like William Shakespeare.

THE KLENCKE ATLAS – This was the largest atlas in the world until 2012 when an even larger atlas, entitled *Earth Platinum,* was created in Australia, .

LADY JANE GREY'S PRAYER BOOK – Small personal books of prayers were often created for wealthy people, so they could carry them wherever they went.

COOKERY BOOKS – The oldest known cookbook in English is *The Forme of Cury* (Cooking), handwritten around 1390, with recipes used in the royal kitchen. The British Library has the first printed copy, published in 1780.

MEDICAL BOOKS – The British Library has works by some of the great forerunners of modern medicine, including Edward Jenner (1749-1823), who invented the word *vaccine* for his anti-smallpox inoculations, Sir James Young Simpson (1811-70), pioneer of anaesthetics, and Joseph Lister (1827-1912), who introduced antiseptic methods in surgery. The discoveries of these men have saved millions of lives.

WILLIAM SHAKESPEARE – The British Library has five precious copies of the First Folio. Out of the 750 that were printed after Shakespeare's death there are thought to be only 233 copies surviving in the world today.

JANE AUSTEN – Though she was one of the greatest romantic novelists, Jane never married. She did, however, become engaged – for just 24 hours. She changed her mind the next day and refused her suitor.

THE BRONTË SISTERS – The Brontë sisters first published their novels under different names so that the publishers and readers would not know they were women. Anne was Acton Bell, Emily was Ellis Bell and Charlotte was Currer Bell. But as their books became bestsellers the sisters revealed their true identities.

THE BROTHERS GRIMM – Their first fairytale collection, *Children's and Household Tales,* was published in 1812. However, the fairy tales the brothers wrote down were not originally told for children. They were told out loud to grown-ups and they could be frightening.

CHARLES DICKENS – Many of Dickens' novels first appeared as serialised chapters, sold in monthly instalments in shops and newsagents. They were hugely popular and people couldn't wait to buy the next episode.

LEONARDO DA VINCI – Leonardo was one of the great artists of his time. His famous portrait, The Mona Lisa, on display at the Louvre in Paris, is still the most valuable painting in the world.

OLIVER GOLDSMITH – Goldsmith wrote on many topics, but he is best-known now as a playwright and as the author of the 1766 novel, *The Vicar of Wakefield.*

CHARLES DARWIN – *On the Origin of Species* rocked the world with its explanation of how life has gradually evolved on our planet over millions of years.

ALICE'S ADVENTURES IN WONDERLAND – There are millions of copies of the 'Alice' books in the world, but the British Library has Lewis Carroll's original manuscript, with his own sketches and notes. The tea party illustration in the collage on page 38 is by Alice's most famous illustrator, John Tenniel.

NEWSPAPERS – The British Library has a copy of every newspaper published every day in Britain and Ireland since 1869, and many more going back to the seventeenth century.

GEORGE FRIDERIC HANDEL – Handel composed operas and oratorios (including *Messiah,* often performed at Christmas) as well as his famous orchestral music. The music of many other great composers is also kept at the British Library.

SHERLOCK HOLMES – Sir Arthur Conan Doyle created many adventures for Sherlock Holmes. The British Library has the first editions of them all.

GLOSSARY

ATLAS – a book of world maps.

BRITISH LIBRARY – the UK's national collection of books and manuscripts.

CHARTER – an agreement in writing between two sets of people, saying what they promise to do for each other.

CONSTITUTION – a set of rules that guides how a country or state works.

EXECUTION – the act of putting someone to death as punishment for a crime.

FOLIO – A book made by folding individual sheets of paper only once. It can also be a term to describe a larger-sized book.

GENTRY – a name traditionally given to people from families of high social standing, who were often rich and owned land or estates.

GOSPELS – the four descriptions of the life and death of Jesus, by St Matthew, St Mark, St Luke and St John, in the New Testament of the Bible.

MOVABLE TYPE – individual letters of the alphabet that could be fitted together to make words and sentences. These were inked up and pressed onto paper, using a printing press.

NOVEL – a long, entertaining, made-up story, usually featuring imaginary people and events.

OLD ENGLISH – the language written and spoken by the Anglo-Saxons up to about 1100.

REVOLUTIONARY – Describes someone or something that changes the way we live or think.

SEAL – A special mark, made in soft wax that then hardens, used by only one person, such as a king, to show that the sealed item comes from him or her.

SHEET MUSIC – handwritten or printed music that shows the melodies, rhythms and chords of a musical piece.

SLEUTH – another name for a detective, someone who solves criminal mysteries.

CREDITS

All photographic images of the books and other works shown in *Books! Books! Books!* are from the British Library archive.